THE CIVIL WAR'S

COMMON SOLDIER

CIVIL WAR SERIES

TEXT BY JAMES I. ROBERTSON, JR.

Additional text by William Marvel

Published by Eastern National Park and Monument Association, copyright 1994.

Eastern National Park & Monument Association aids and promotes the historical, scientific and educational activities of the National Park Service. It also supports research, interpretation and conservation programs of the Service. As a nonprofit cooperating association recognized by Congress, it makes interpretive material available to park visitors and the general public.

Cover: "Emblems of Valor," painting by Don Troiani. Photograph courtesy Historical Art Prints, Ltd., Southbury, Connecticut.

Back cover: Painting by Mark Kaufman, 203 Brandywine Blvd., Wilmington, DE

Printed on recycled paper.

THE CIVIL WAR'S COMMON SOLDIER

*T*he American Civil War, like all such uprisings, was slow in conception and subtle in development. Political commissions and omissions lay at the roots of the explosion. The existence of slavery in a new nation that proclaimed liberty for all, the role of the previously sovereign states in a central government yet to be clearly defined, the growing industrial might of the North competing more and more with the "Cotton Kingdom" agriculture of the South, a general lack of understanding and communication between the sections of a country that was a United States in name only—these were the major issues that neither time nor statesmen could resolve. So in December 1860, the shouting turned to shooting, the politician gave way to the soldier, and war replaced uncertainty.

In a conflict that was the largest in the history of the Western Hemisphere, the Civil War brought unprecedented suffering in every form. Yet the greatest tragedy of all was that both sides were fighting for the same thing: America, as North and South each envisioned what the still-ripening republic should be.

Young men of the Union and Confederacy alike went to war to defend the same Constitution. A Louisiana recruit wrote in June 1861 that he and his friends were Confederate soldiers because "the Magna Carta of liberties, the constitution," had "fallen entirely into the hands of [Northern] fanatics." Another Confederate put it succinctly: "We are fighting for the Constitution that our forefathers made, and not as old Abe would have it." A few

CONFEDERATE SOL-
DIERS OF COMPANY D,
3RD GEORGIA INFANTRY.

(MC)

1

months later, an Ohio private asserted that "the strength of the nation is to be tried here, whether we have a country or not; whether our constitution is a rope of sand, that it may be severed wherever it is smote."

In America's eighth decade, preserving the Union and preserving a way of life had somehow become incompatible ideals. The most effective motivation for Northern recruits was "the Union" and all that it denoted. Many remembered their grandparents relating thrilling stories of the 1770s and the fight for American independence. Again and again in the letters of Billy Yanks, one encounters the phrase "fighting to maintain the best government on earth."

Southerners saw the outbreak of civil war in a different light. A North Carolinian explained: "The Southern States passed ordinances of secession for the purpose of withdrawing from a partnership in which the majority were oppressing the minority, and we simply asked 'to be let alone.'"

Protection of home and hearth also became fundamental aims of both sides. One Southern enlistee in 1861 explained why he was joining the army: "If we are conquered we will be driven penniless and dishonored from the land of our birth. . . . As I have often said I had rather fall in this cause than to live to see my country dismantled of its glory and independence—for of its honor it cannot be deprived."

A Wisconsin private felt essentially the same way two years later. To his sweetheart he wrote: "Home is sweet and friends are dear, but what would they all be to let the country go in ruin, and be a slave. . . . I know that I am doing my duty, and I know that it is my duty to do as I am now a-doing. If I live to get back, I shall be

proud of the freedom I shall have, and know that I helped to gain that freedom. If I should not get back, it will do them good that do get back."

In 1861 tens of thousands of American youths on both sides rushed to answer the call to arms. They became soldiers because they had been caught up in the heated atmosphere and angry words of the day, or they had been emotionally moved by swaying oratory, inspiring music, patriotic slogans, the sight of a flag waving defiantly in the air. Youthful innocence and dreamy passion swept them onward. A Confederate veteran later recalled: "I was a mere boy [in 1861] and carried away by boyish enthusiasm. I was tormented by a feverish anxiety before I joined my regiment for fear the fighting would be over before I got into it."

Those recruits were ready to fight, but few of them knew how to fight. The War of 1812 was history, the Mexican War a vague childhood recollection to most of the youths drawn into the struggle of the 1860s. They had no conception of drill, life in the open, following orders unhesitatingly, mastering weapons, digging earthworks, and eating unfamiliar food. They would confront the novelty of living in company with thousands of strangers. They would face diseases they had never known and wounds they had never imagined. And through it all, these common-folk-turned-

soldiers would endure homesickness to a degree none of them had ever envisioned.

About 3,000,000 soldiers fought in the Civil War, with the North having a 2 to 1 ratio. The men of blue and gray were far more alike than unalike. Mostly products of rural backgrounds, they spoke the same language and shared the same heritage. They had common hopes; they endured common hardships. The majority of soldiers knew the basic rudiments of reading and writing. Billy Yanks tended to be better educated because most Northern states had better school systems. In some units formed in the rural South, illiteracy was pronounced. Thirty-six of 72 privates in one North Carolina company made a mark rather than a signature at the muster-in; 27 of 100 recruits in another Tarheel company did the same.

Johnny Rebs and Billy Yanks were also highly independent-minded. They went off to war as citizen-soldiers: volunteers who tended to remain more citizen than soldier. Very seldom did these men became fully regimented and militarized. Many of them retained in large measure an ignorance of army life and an indifference to army discipline. In camp, on the march, and in battle, they fought with a looseness

that no amount of training could remove. Soldiers on both sides demonstrated that they could be led but they could not be driven; and any officer who attempted the latter was bound to encounter at least resistance and at most rebellion. The individualism of the Civil War's common soldiers was but a reflection of the societies that spawned them.

Typical human beings in mid-nineteenth century America, the army volunteers of North and South performed as one might expect. Many of them became outstanding soldiers, some of them had rather poor records, a few were shirkers and cowards; most of them, however, were just average. Yet for four horrible years those representatives of the nation's common folk bore on their shoulders the heaviest responsibilities that have ever been placed on the people of this land. And they carried that burden so well that we still marvel at their strength and endurance.

Their story is a mixture of hardship, humor, and heroism—which are doubtless the ways in which Johnny Rebs and Billy Yanks would like to be remembered.

On enlistment, a man's physical condition received little attention from contract surgeons or anyone else in attendance. Then came about two weeks in which recruits at a rendezvous camp went through the awkward process of learning the basic rudiments of camp life, drill, and the use of arms. By the end of that period, the various companies were organized into regiments.

The clothing and equipment distributed to each recruit might have seemed bulky to Northern soldiers, who tended to be abundantly supplied at the outset. Confederate enlistees often had to rely on individual efforts to clothe and equip them-

RECRUITING OFFICE OF NINTH MASSACHUSETTS BATTERY, BOSTON, 1862.

(LC)

selves. One Virginian wrote with assurance: "Wisdom is born of experience, and before many campaigns have been worried through the private soldier, reduced to the minimum, consisted of one man, one hat, one jacket, one pair pants, one pair draws, one pair socks, and his baggage was one blanket, one gum-cloth, and one haversack."

Regulation uniforms were dark blue for the North and light gray for the South. However, cloth—like everything else—quickly became scarce in the embattled Confederacy. The principal source for Southern soldier apparel soon became captured Union uniforms. Johnny Rebs sought to alter the color by dying the clothing in a mixture of walnut hulls, acorns, and lye. This changed the tint to a light tan which Southerners labeled "butternut."

The introduction to government-issue attire could be a shock. Federal uniforms came in four basic sizes. A New England recruit saw a messmate "so tightly buttoned [that] it seemed doubtful if he could draw another breath." Over in the 10th Rhode Island, a soldier told of a friend who was less than five feet tall: "His first pair of army drawers reached to his chin. This he considers very economical, as it saves the necessity of shirts."

Of course, with some troops no quality of clothing and equipment could improve their appearance. In 1863 Louisiana soldier Robert Newell watched

4

400 Texas Rangers ride into camp. Newell was repulsed at the sight. "If the Confederacy has no better soldiers than those we are in A bad roe for stumps, for they looke more like Baboons mounted on gotes than anything else."

Quite often, at the end of basic training, a local delegation (dominated largely by women) bestowed an ornate flag upon the regiment. The lady presenting the standard would implore the men in a flowery speech to love their country and to fight for it with their lives. Accepting

SOLDIERS OF THE 23RD PENNSYLVANIA.

(USAMHI)

tion to do the honors. The man, a bit nervous at the starring role he was to have, fortified himself beforehand with a drink, then another, and another. He managed to stumble to the speaker's stand, and he somehow got through his address in a halting manner. Then, momentarily oblivious to everything, he proceeded to give the same speech all over again—after which he sat down and cried, to the mortification of the ladies and to the amusement of the soldiers.

Proud recruits who left for war had strong opinions about the shirkers who remained behind. Private Henry Bear of Illinois gave a typical expression. From camp in Tennessee, Bear instructed his wife: "You must tell evry man of Doubtful Loyalty for me, up ther in the north, that he is meaner than any son of a bitch in hell. I would rather shoot one of them a great deal more than one [Southerner] living here."

Unique regiments abounded on both sides during the Civil War. The 1st New York, under Colonel Elmer Ellsworth, was recruited largely from the New York Fire Department ranks and was known to contain several dangerous criminals. The

PRESENTATION OF A REGIMENTAL FLAG ON BEHALF OF THE LADIES OF BOSTON.

(LC)

the flag, an officer would respond with an equally glowing address pledging that his men would never disgrace the sacred banner.

On more than one occasion, a foulup made this ceremony ludicrous. Such was the case the afternoon the women of Fayetteville gave a flag to the 43rd North Carolina. None of the good ladies was willing to make the presentation speech, so they invited a local orator of some reputa-

average age of all officers and men in the 23rd Pennsylvania was nineteen. In contrast was the 37th Iowa, known as the "Graybeard Regiment" because all recruits for this home guard unit had to be at least forty-five years of age.

Faculty from the Illinois State Normal College so dominated the 33rd Illinois that it was known as the "Teacher's Regiment." Its officers were often accused of refusing to obey any order that was not absolutely correct in grammar and syntax. The "Iowa Temperance Regiment" gained its sobriquet because its entire membership vowed that it would "touch not, taste not, handle not spirituous or malt liquor, wine or cider." Some of the Iowans later in the war violated the pledge, but they were excused on the grounds that "it has only been at such times as they were under the overruling power of military necessity."

Civil War armies were young in composition. Ages ranged from lads with smooth faces to old men with gray beards. The largest single age group was eighteen, followed by soldiers twenty-one and nineteen. Unknown numbers of children served in the armies. Edward Black was nine years old when he entered an Indiana regiment. Among the youngest Confederate soldiers was Charles C. Hay, who joined an Alabama regiment at the age of eleven. John Mather Sloan of Texas lost a leg in battle at the age of thirteen.

The most famous of the dozens of young drummer boys was Johnny Clem of Newark, Ohio. He went to war at the age of ten. In Clem's first battle, a shell fragment ripped his drum apart. He became known as "Johnny Shiloh." Gallantry in action two years later brought him promotion to sergeant. Clem made the army a

career, and he retired in 1916 with the rank of major general.

Three "boys" had extraordinary careers in the Civil War. Pennsylvania's Galusha Pennypacker received promotion to brigadier general a month before his twenty-first birthday. William P. Roberts became the Confederacy's youngest general at the age of twenty-three. Arthur MacArthur, father of the famed World War II commander, won the Congressional Medal of Honor at Missionary Ridge, Tennessee, while only eighteen. Months later, MacArthur became colonel of the 24th Wisconsin, and after the war he rose to lieutenant general in the army.

At the other end of the age spectrum was Curtis King, who served four months in the 37th Iowa before being discharged for

disability. King was eighty. One of the oldest of the Confederates was E. Pollard. In the summer of 1862, the 73-year-old North Carolinian enlisted as a substitute. Pollard was shortly discharged "for rheumatism and old age."

Civil War soldiers came in every size. The shortest serviceman was from Ohio and stood 3 feet, 4 inches tall. In contrast, David Van Buskirk of Indiana was 6 feet, 11 inches in height. Van Buskirk had a ready reply for those who gawked openly at his stature. When he left for war, he would say, each of his six sisters "leaned down and kissed me on top of the head."

Occupations of the soldiers were not as varied as would exist in a troop call-up today. A survey of 9,000 Civil War soldier occupations contained 5,600 farmers. The next vocations were students (474), laborers (472), and clerks (321). Some of the remaining occupations given were unique. One man termed himself a rogue, another listed his status as convict, and several recruits put down their occupation as "gentleman."

The greatest flood of immigration in the nation's history occurred in the decades just

before the Civil War. New England and the Midwest became home for the vast majority of those new citizens. As a result, one of every five Billy Yanks was foreign-born. In contrast, one of every twenty Johnny Rebs was born outside the country. Every nationality had representatives in the Civil War.

No foreign group on either side in the war gained greater renown—positively as well as negatively—than the Irish. They quickly earned a reputation for overindulgence in whiskey and an overfondness for fighting, whether it be the enemy or them-

lows did have. They got into a row about putting up their tents and had a free for all fight and were knocking each other over the head with pick handles, tent poles, and any thing they got hold of. Pretty soon their Colonel, O Marah, came out of his tent with a great wide bladed broadsword that is said to have belonged to some of his ancestors. And the way he did bast those Irish fellows with the flat of it was a caution. He stopped the row, and they settled down. His Regiment adore him."

selves. To an Indiana soldier stationed near Vicksburg in 1863, the arrival of some reinforcements was hardly reassuring. "The 90th Ill., the Irish Regiment," he wrote in his diary, "came into camp just back of us this morning. And such a time as those fellows did have.

Felix Brannigan of the 75th New York offered a personal explanation of how he and his fellow Irishmen thought. "As we rush on with the tide of battle, severe sense of fear is swallowed up in the wild joy we feel thrilling thro every fibre of our system. . . . There is an elasticity in the Irish temperament which enables its possessor to boldly stare Fate in the face, and laugh at all the reverses of fortune . . . and crack a joke with as much glee in the heat of battle as in the social circle by the winter fire."

Germans, Italians, Englishmen, and Canadians also served in large numbers with the Union armies. Union encampments often sounded like "a babel of tongues." A Mississippi surgeon once listened to a long line of Union prisoners pass. He then turned to a colleague and said despairingly: "Pierce, we are fighting the world."

Representatives of fifteen different countries served in one New York regiment. Fortunate it was that the Hungarian colonel of the unit could give

Germans, Italians, Englishmen, and Canadians also served in large numbers with the Union armies. Union encampments often sounded like "a babel of tongues."

A POOR MAN'S FIGHT

by William Marvel

Initial response to President Lincoln's call for troops proved so enthusiastic that all the volunteers could not be accommodated. Men were turned away whom the government would have welcomed two years later, and in April of 1862 the War Department actually closed its recruiting offices. Within weeks it became evident that this was a mistake, and the summer of that year saw massive enlistment drives, but by autumn the reservoir of purely patriotic recruits had been effectively exhausted.

The U.S. government answered this lapse with financial inducements and the threat of conscription. Since the early months of the war, volunteers had been rewarded with a bounty of $100, most of which was deferred until the soldier was honorably discharged, but the bounty seems to have been a significant lure for men from poorer families. The Militia Act of 1862 required individual states to draft men if their enlistment quotas fell short, and in the spring of 1863 Congress passed the first national con-

scription law, authorizing the central government to select reluctant recruits. In 1863 the federal bounty was also increased to $300, in an effort to boost volunteering and reduce the number of men who might have to be drafted. The men who responded to these bounties hailed principally from the lower economic strata of society.

The Conscription Act of 1863 also permitted two means of escape for those drafted men who could not obtain an exemption for health or hardship. Anyone who paid a commutation fee of $300—the yearly wage of a common laborer—would be excused from the draft call in which he was chosen, though he might be drafted again in the next levy. The man who wished to secure permanent exemption could simply hire someone who was willing to enlist as a substitute in his place. These clauses, and particularly the commutation provision, provoked many to object that the conflict was "a rich man's war, but a poor man's fight."

The same complaint arose in the South, which instituted a national draft months earlier than the North. Confederate conscription began in April of 1862, and that law

also allowed the hiring of substitutes. While it permitted no one to buy his way out of service with a cash payment, the Southern draft did excuse men on other grounds, most notably for the ownership of a certain number of slaves: that number was changed during the war, from twenty to fifteen, but it was never reduced to a level consistent with moderate economic status. As late as the summer of 1864, when Confederate manpower had ebbed critically, the owner of fifteen slaves could also pay what amounted to a commutation fee of several hundred dollars to retain the services of one white overseer.

State and local government officials were also exempted from Confederate service. In Georgia, for instance, Howell Cobb complained in 1864 that the governor suffered thousands of justices of the peace, court clerks, sheriffs, and deputies to continue in office when the limited business of the courts would permit all those officials to be replaced by far fewer men who were over the military age. Thousands of other political favorites had also received exemptions through militia commissions, Cobb charged. The Richmond govern-

orders in seven different tongues. Scandinavians were especially visible in units from the upper Midwest. The 15th Wisconsin was predominantly Norwegian. Identity in the unit must have been a problem, for 128 men had the first name of Ole and in one company were five men named Ole Olsen.

Civil War soldiers in the early stages of the war went into the army under the twin motivations of patriotism and enthusiasm. They were volunteers and proud of it. Yet they proved insufficient in numbers to satisfy the demands of a rapidly burgeon-

ment offered only token bounties to its volunteers, but in the North the bounty system expanded with each successive draft call. The federal bounty of $300 was frequently augmented by state, county, and town bounties as these municipalities competed for the dwindling supply of men willing to serve. In some communities volunteers could demand $800 or more just from town officials who dreaded a draft of local citizens, and many towns paid the commutation fee for their drafted residents—or funded the cost of substitutes, after the obnoxious commutation clause was eliminated. By the autumn of 1864 an enlistment could bring as much as $1,200 to $1,500 dollars.

Ironically, more of the poorest volunteers had already responded to the lower bounties of 1862, and it was they who did most of the fighting. The bigger bounties of the war's final months tended to draw more affluent recruits who might not have volunteered at all without the prospect of such a windfall, and few of these later troops suffered any of the privations or dangers endured by their predecessors.

While wealthy and politically connected Southerners frequently managed to avoid mili-

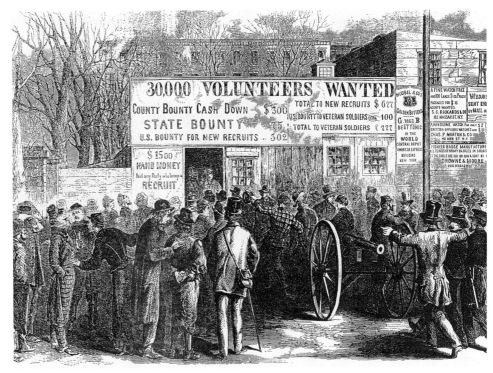

tary service through the entire war, their poorer neighbors usually escaped conscription only by physical flight. The mountains of Virginia, Kentucky, Tennessee, and the Carolinas teemed with deserters and draft evaders, and thousands of Confederate troops had to be diverted to hunt for them, or to curb their depredations. Isolated regions of Mississippi, Alabama, and Florida also hosted whole communities of fugitives. Northern officials complained of similarly troublesome enclaves

in the Midwest or along the Canadian border, to which many draft-age Union citizens fled as a last resort.

For all the incentives and coercion employed to mobilize armies North and South, it was the early volunteers who bore the brunt of the war on both sides. Despite the intellectuals, professionals, and planter aristocrats who so prominently officered the legions blue and gray, it was those of the least means who more often shed their blood and sweat.

"RECRUITING FOR THE WAR" ILLUSTRATION FROM FRANK LESLIE'S *ILLUSTRATED NEWSPAPER*, MARCH 1864.

(LC)

ing war. Hence, in April 1862, the Confederate States of America enacted the first conscription act in American history. The Union followed suit eleven months later. Men forced into the armies by conscription were suspect in loyalty and behavior. As a result, officers entrusted with getting them to their units often transported the recruits as if they were prisoners of war. A veteran New England soldier looked at one bunch of conscripts arriving at the front and snorted that "such another, depraved, vice-hardened and desperate set of human beings never before disgraced an

army." When a similar group joined Confederate General Robert E. Lee's army in 1864, a Virginia artillerist commented: "Some of them looked like they had been resurrected from the grave, after laying therein for twenty years or more."

In too many instances as well, a different kind of enlistee came forth in the latter half of the war. Some joined to escape the onus of being termed conscripts; others entered the service under pressure from relatives and friends. An officer in the 70th Indiana sneered early in 1863 that nine-tenths of the new recruits "enlisted just

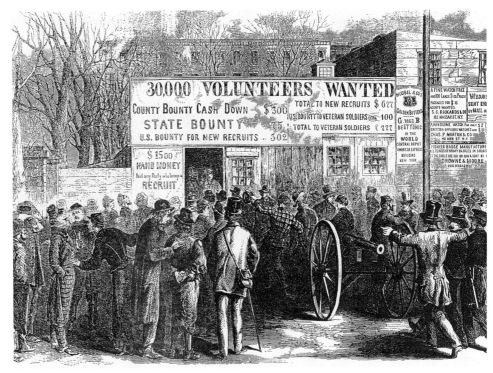

FREEMEN!
AVOID CONSCRIPTION!

The undersigned desires to raise a Company for the Confederate States service, and for that purpose I call upon the people of the Counties of Jefferson and Hawkins, Tenn., to meet promptly at Russellville, on SATURDAY, JULY 19th, 1862, and organize a Company.

By so doing you will avoid being taken as Conscripts, for that Act will now be enforced by order of the War Department. Rally, then, my Countrymen, to your Country's call.

S. M. DENNISON,
Of the Confederate States Army.

CHARLESTON, Tenn., JUNE 30, 1862.

THIS POSTER URGED SOUTHERNERS TO "AVOID CONSCRIPTION."

(LC)

A Louisiana private in camp near his home solemnly informed his wife: "Dont never come here as long as you can ceep away, for you will smell hell here." An Alabama recruit asked his brother to visit him in camp, but to bring a shotgun with him for his own protection.

Camp shelters varied with the supply and the season. In warm weather or on the march, most soldiers preferred to sleep in the open to take advantage of any breeze. For inclement weather, tents were far more available on the Union side. Yet there never seemed to be enough for the number of men in need of them.

Three basic types of canvas shelters existed at the time of the Civil War. The largest was the Sibley tent, bell-shaped and supported by an upright center pole. It could hold as many as twenty soldiers at a time—so long as they slept in position like the spokes of a wheel, with feet to the center and heads toward the tent edge. The "A" or wedge tent had a horizontal ridge pole and was tall enough to accommodate a man in standing position. This was a favorite type with officers. By the end of

because somebody else was going, and the other tenth was ashamed to stay at home."

Every Civil War soldier had something to say about camp life—and it was generally negative. An Ohio volunteer expressed shock at the lack of morals in his camp. "I shall try to come out of the army as I went into it—a Christian Man," he reassured his father, "but I can hardly describe it to you the temptation and wickedness w'h surrounds a man in camp: Drinking, Swearing, & Gambling is carried on among Officers and men from the highest to the lowest."

SIBLEY, WALL, AND "A" TENTS AT FEDERAL ENCAMPMENT AT CUMBERLAND LANDING, VIRGINIA.

(LC)

the war, the dog tent was the most popular shelter. Designed for two men, it too had a horizontal crossbar at the top but was much more shallow than the wedge tent.

When armies went into winter quarters, troops on both sides constructed two kinds of dwellings. One was "bombproofs," consisting of excavations

"BOMBPROOF" QUAR-
TERS OF MEN IN FORT
SEDGWICK, ALSO KNOWN
AS FORT HELL.

(LC)

with roofs built a foot or two above ground level. Most soldiers spent the cold months in log huts reminiscent of the homes of frontier pioneers. Often soldiers gave their winter shacks a bit of individualism by affixing boards over the entrance with house-names scrawled thereon. "Growlers," "Buzzard Roost," "Sans Souci," and names of famous hotels were among the favorites.

Homesickness, foul weather, filth, crime, lack of privacy, stern discipline, and a general absence of godliness quickly produced criticisms of life in camp. Further, oppressive heat and stifling humidity prevailed during the months of campaigning; mosquitoes and flies swarmed at every movement; every army

camp in the field had an overpowering stench because of lack of attention given to latrine procedures and garbage pits. Drinking water was not always plentiful; when available, it tended to be muddy and warm.

The winter months were the worst time for many troops. Inactivity and boredom prevailed. Soldiers no longer found jokes funny. Manners of compatriots that once were comical became contemptuous. Conversations lagged simply because the limited subjects had been exhausted. Discipline became strained as men balked at officers whom they disliked more with each passing week. Tempers, resentment, and impatience ran high. Surprisingly large numbers of soldiers actually came to look forward to springtime and battle as a relief from the dreary and despairing routine of winter quarters.

Homesickness, foul weather, filth, crime, lack of privacy, stern discipline, and a general absence of godliness quickly produced criticisms of life in camp.

FEDERAL SOLDIERS AT
WINTER QUARTERS.

(LC)

Officers sought to get around the negatives of camp life by keeping the men as busy as possible. This meant drill, drill, and more drill, especially during the first months in the army. The main exercises which new units practiced were learning to do turns and facings while standing still and marching, performing the simple rudiments of close-formation drill, the proper handling of arms, and similar routines. Men learned how to salute amid stern commands from sergeants to stand erect. New soldiers struggled with the intricacies of loading weapons "by the numbers." For some, it was an education; for others, it was total chaos.

Even the simplest of army maneuvers was a problem for many enlisted men who were untutored farmboys with an ignorance even of the difference between their left and right feet. A Pennsylvania enlistee remarked on his first day's attempt at drill that "when the order 'Right face!' was given, face met face in inquiring astonishment, and frantic attempts to obey the order properly made still greater confusion."

One exasperated Georgian swore to a companion that "if he lived to see the close of this war he meant to get two pups and name one of them 'fall in' and the other 'close up' and as soon as they were old enough to know their names right well he intended to shoot them both, and thus put

an end to 'fall in' and 'close up.'"

Marches were also considered a necessary part of drill, and they tended to be a sore trial in every sense. In the mountains of western Virginia during the war's first summer, Private John Hollway recounted a march to his Georgia sweetheart: "We slept on the ground for four nights with only one blanket apiece, and what was the worst thing that happened to me was that in going up the mountains I lost one of my shoes in the mud and it was so dark that I could not find it and then of course I had to carry one until I came back to camp. You must wonder at soldiers having to do without shoes and blankets sometimes. I believe men can stand most anything after they get used to it. The hardest part is getting used to it."

Private Ted Barclay of the 4th Virginia seconded that belief. Following a severe march in the war's first winter, Barclay jokingly informed his sister: "Well, here I am at the old camp near Winchester, broken down, halt, lame, blind, crippled, and whatever else you can think of—but I am still kicking."

Since the majority of officers and men were starting out the Civil War as novices (the U.S. Army numbered but 16,000 men at the outbreak of the war), drill was often akin to the ignorant leading the uneducated. Green officers giving correct instruc-

tions while scores of men were attempting to maintain lines and proper cadence could be nerve-racking. It was for Captain Daniel G. Chandler, who was marching his company one day when the men began rapidly approaching a fence. Chandler could not think of the proper command to give; and the closer the company got to the fence, the less Chandler's thinking processes functioned. Finally the frantic captain bellowed: "Gentlemen, will you please halt!"

Little sympathy existed down in the ranks for unknowledgeable superiors. The greener the officer appeared, the more difficult time he had at the outset with his men. A young and thoroughly inexperienced lieutenant was assigned to a new company of rough-hewn soldiers. The lieutenant was small, seemingly inept, and weak of voice. When he rode out in front of his troops for the first time, out of the ranks came a shout: "And a little child shall lead them!" Raucous laughter followed.

DRESS REHEARSAL OF COMPANY K, 4TH REGIMENT, GEORGIA VOLUNTEER INFANTRY.

(PHOTO COURTESY OF GEORGIA DEPT. OF ARCHIVES AND HISTORY)

The column came to a stop only a few feet from the barrier. Chandler then shouted: "Gentlemen, we will now take a recess of ten minutes. And when you fall in, will you please reform on the other side of the fence!"

Late in July 1861, the 3rd Iowa had one of its first dress parades. A private in the unit confided in his journal that "the new Adjutant Laffingwell acted most supremely awkward. The whole Regiment as far as I noticed, was amused. I could hardly keep a straight face. Take the Major's blunders together with the adjutant's, and the parade tonight was a fizzle."

The officer calmly went about the day's duties. Early the next morning the men were aroused from sleep by an order to prepare for an all-day march. The announcement ended: "And a little child shall lead them—on a damned big horse!"

In the first weeks of any unit's training, accidents with weapons were so commonplace as to be inevitable. Cavalrymen drilling with sabers regularly pricked their mounts and frightened the horses into stampedes. Recruits trying to master the basics of artillery fared little better. Gunners in a Massachusetts battery one quiet day decided to test their marksmanship at a large tree on a hilltop 1,000 yards away. They clumsily set the sights at 1,600 yards and almost annihilated a village on the other side of the hill.

Even though the bayonet was rarely used in combat (less than half of 1 percent of Civil War battle wounds resulted from blade weapons), drills with the weapon were an integral part of camp life. The exercises were apparently wondrous to behold, if a New Hampshire soldier's account is reliable. He watched his regiment go through the various steps and lunges. To him the troops looked "like a line of beings made up about equally of the frog, the sand-hill crane, the sentinel crab, and the grasshopper; all of them rapidly jumping, thrusting, swinging, striking, jerking every which way, and all gone stark mad."

And then, of course, there was the musket, which was the most important item in a soldier's equipment. Nevertheless, mobilization of troops too often occurred before units could receive their arms. The 77th Ohio left for war completely unarmed. At the first major engagement in the western theater, the 16th Iowa arrived on the field with muskets but without its first issue of ammunition.

The Union armies initially used eighty-one types of muskets. They ranged in caliber from .45 to .75, and several models antedated the War of 1812. Soldiers for understandable reasons called the larger caliber guns "mules" and "pumpkin

slingers." When a man prepared to shoot one of these antiquated pieces, he gripped the weapon as hard as he could, braced himself as tensely as possible, took aim, shut his eyes tightly, and then pulled the trigger.

A number of new Union regiments received huge .69 caliber smoothbores which had been popular for generations. An Iowa newspaperman examined a shipment of these blunderbusses and concluded: "I think it would be a master stroke of policy to allow the [Confederates] to steal them. They are the old-fashioned-brass-mounted-and-of-such-is-the-kingdom-of-Heaven kind that are infinitely more dangerous to friend than enemy—will kick further than they will shoot."

UNION SOLDIER POSES WITH MUSKET AND BAYONET.

(USAMHI)

"A YANKEE VOLUNTEER" SKETCH BY EDWIN FORBES.

(LC)

"A SOLDIER'S DREAM OF HOME" LITHOGRAPH PUBLISHED BY CURRIER AND IVES.

(LC)

The .577 caliber Springfield rifle-musket was the most prevalent shoulder arm of the Civil War. Next in popularity was the English-made and extremely similar Enfield. Yet the general prohibition against firing live ammunition for practice, the tendency of all soldiers to aim high, and the heavy smoke from the gunpowder of that day reduced accuracy in battle to a minimum. One authority on logistics asserted that each Johnny Reb and Billy Yank on an average expended 900 rounds of lead and 240 pounds of powder in taking out one of the enemy.

During the two-thirds or three-fourths of each year when the men of blue and gray were in camp, morale underwent severe testing. Late in 1862, Constantine Hege of the 48th North Carolina confessed to his parents: "Would to God this war might end with the close of the year and we could all enjoy the blessings of comfortable house and home one time more. I never knew how to value home until I came in the army."

Furloughs were rare commodities in Civil War armies, largely because of the distance and time involved in a man getting to and from home. Confederate General D. H. Hill advocated greater leniency in the granting of leaves. "If our brave soldiers are not occasionally permitted to visit their homes," he warned, "the next generation in the South will be composed of the descendants of skulkers and cowards."

Applications for leave flowed steadily through any regimental headquarters. Most of them were denied. However, in December 1863, a Maine sergeant used a distinctive approach. He justified his petition on the basis of holy scripture, citing Deuteronomy 20:7: "And what man is there that have betrothed a wife, and hath not taken her? Let him go and return unto his house, lest he die in the battle, and another man take her." The strategy worked: the sergeant spent Christmas at home.

Soldiers' letters, diaries, and reminiscences make it clear that a constant search occurred for diversions to overcome the tedium and monotony of army routine.

Neither government was of any assistance in this regard. Unlike today, no army service agencies, post exchanges, lounges, or libraries existed for the men; telephones, radio, television, and movies, of course, were unknown; newspapers were a rarity in camp. Few entertainment groups ever visited troops in the field. In sum, the soldiers were left to themselves to combat their own loneliness.

That explains why letter-writing was the most popular occupation of soldiers. It is only during war that the plain people become articulate to a degree comparable to the upper classes. Johnny Rebs and Billy Yanks wrote about camp life, battles, sickness, the weather, and anything else they had seen or thought. Interspersed throughout the letters would be questions about conditions back home: the health of family members, the progress of the crops, and the like. Some of the letters were models of literary excellence; others were so badly composed, especially with phonetic spelling, as to be impossible to translate. The great majority of Civil War letters lay between those extremes, with tendencies toward the more illiterate side.

In October 1861, Private Charles Futch told his brother, who was serving in another unit: "John I want you to write to me more plainer than you have bin a writing." Charles added that he had carried a bundle of John's letters through two regiments but that "they was not a man that could even read the date of the month."

An Alabama soldier likewise rebuked his wife mildly for her handwriting. "I had not a like to maid out half of yourre words," he informed her. "theare is some that I hant maid out yet."

When a Federal army was undergoing reorganization, a Billy Yank stated: "They are deviding the army up into corpses." Medical terms always proved troublesome for many writers. "Tifoid feaver" was a better-than-usual rendition for one of the war's most dreaded diseases. Pneumonia once appeared as "new mornion," and hospital was often "horse pittle." The most prevalent of all soldier illnesses, diarrhea, produced the greatest variety of spellings. One Union soldier got both his spelling and his meaning confused when he told his wife: "I am well at the present with the exception I have got the Dyerear and I hope these lines will find you the same."

A letter was the sole contact with loved ones. One soldier stated to his cousin: "I never thought so much of letters

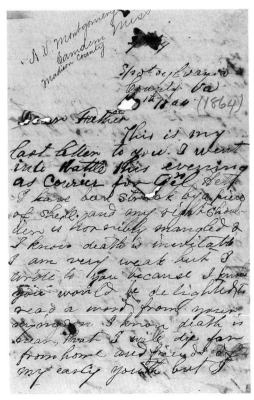

as I have since I have been here. The monotony of camp life would be almost intolerable were it not for these friendly letters." A Connecticut private expressed a similar sentiment more dramatically: "The soldier looks upon a letter from home as a perfect God send—sent as it were, by some kind ministering Angel Spirit, to cheer his dark and weary hours."

UNION OFFICERS OF COMPANY C, 1ST CONNECTICUT ARTILLERY.

(LC)

This was also the first time in American history that so large a percentage of the common folk had been pulled away from home. Soldiers were seeing new things and living in an unusual environment. They were in a flashing, strange world whose sights they wished to share with the homefolk. So they wrote letters—tens of thousands of them—and they commented on every possible subject with oftentimes pointed language.

A young Billy Yank described his first encounter with the enemy in a direct and forceful way. "Dear Pa," he wrote, "Went out a Skouting yesterday. We got to one house where there were five secessionists, they broke & run and Arch holored out to shoot the ornery suns of biches and wee all let go at them. They may say what they please, but godamit Pa it is fun."

Less-than-pleasant campsites always provoked sharp observations. One foot soldier summarized the sparseness of his regiment's surroundings and concluded: "To tell the truth we are between sh-t and a sweat out here." At the same time, men in the ranks were especially sensitive to unfavorable home front gossip. In June 1864, young John Evans responded to alleged criticism in his community by writing his wife: "The people that speaks slack about me may kiss my ass. Mollie, excuse the vulgar language if you please."

Far more pleasing to the soldiers than writing home was hearing from home. Mail call took precedence over anything, including food. It was the only tonic for the chronic homesickness that plagued most men of blue and gray. In March 1863, a soldier told his wife that he "was almost down with histericks to hear from home," and later in the war, when a Minnesota private at last received a letter from his family, he confessed: "I can never remember of having been so glad

MEMBERS OF "RICHMOND GRAYS" ARTILLERY.

(MC)

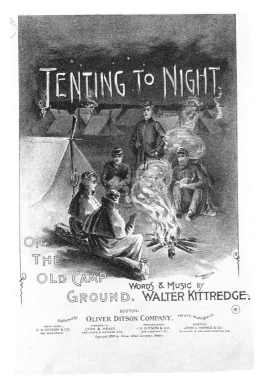

major reason why the conflict of the 1860s sparked more new songs than any other event in American history. The first Civil War song appeared three days after the firing on Fort Sumter started the struggle. Four years later, over 2,000 melodies had been added to the national heritage and to denominational hymnbooks.

Among the best-known songs were "Dixie," "The Battle Hymn of the Republic," "The Yellow Rose of Texas," "Marching Along," "Listen to the Mocking Bird," "When Johnny Comes Marching Home Again," "Yankee Doodle," "Pop Goes the Weasel," "Maryland My Maryland," "Aura Lee," "Sweet Evalina," and "The Battle Cry of Freedom." Favorite hymns were "Amazing Grace," "Rock of Ages," "Nearer My God to Thee," "How Firm a Foundation," "Praise God from Whom All Blessings Flow," "All Hail the Power of Jesus's Name," and "O God Our Help in Ages Past."

before. I sat down and cried with joy and thankfulness."

More than American servicemen of any other age, Civil War troops were singing soldiers. Next to letter-writing, music was the most popular diversion in the army. Men left for war with a song on their lips; they sang while marching or waiting behind breastworks; they hummed melodies moving into battle; music swelled from every nighttime bivouac. That is the

The truly popular tunes in camp were not stirring airs that folks back home—and generations of Americans thereafter—sang inspirationally. The soldiers' favorites of the Civil War were songs of the heart and soul:

"When This Cruel War Is Over," "All Quiet along the Potomac," "Tenting Tonight on the Old Camp Ground," "Auld Lang Syne," and the most endearing of all war songs, "Home Sweet Home."

Regimental bands were few, which may have been a blessing. The scarcity of instruments, the limited talent among band members (more than one colonel "punished" soldiers for misdemeanors by assigning them to the band), and weariness from campaigning often resulted in inferior renditions of the most simple tunes. Fortunately, in any sizable group of soldiers could be found at least a banjo player, a fiddler, or a man proficient with the Jew's harp. That sufficed to keep men entertained with such foot-stomping melodies as "Arkansas Traveler," "Billy in the Low Grounds," and "Hell Broke Loose in Georgia."

Civil War soldiers tended to be habitual teasers. Practical jokes and barbed one-liners were the favorite weapons. Covering a chimney top so that the occupants of the hut would be smoked out was a regular practice. Terrifying a recruit on his first nighttime picket duty by impersonating ghosts was an enjoyable but potentially dangerous prank. Loading firewood with gunpowder produced some spectacular displays in camp.

Visitors to an encampment were favorite targets for the jibes of soldiers. In a rare instance, the civilian might enjoy the last laugh. Men in the 7th Virginia one quiet day spied an elderly minister, long white beard flowing in the wind, riding into camp. A good-natured Virginian immediately called out: "Look out, boys! Here comes Father Abraham!"

"Young men," the cleric replied quietly when the chortles subsided, "you are mistaken. I am Saul, the son of Kish, searching for his father's asses, and I have found them."

Physical contests were a regular part of camp life. Boxing, broad-jumping, wrestling matches, foot-races, hurdles, and sometimes free-for-all scuffles all were popular pastimes. Of the competitive sports, none gained more popularity during the war years than a new game called baseball. The ball was then softer, but the base runner was out only when hit by a thrown or

batted ball. High scores were therefore the general rule. A Massachusetts regiment once trounced a New York unit by a 62–20 score. The Texas Rangers loved the sport and played whenever possible for about six months. They gave up baseball because of Frank Ezell. A burly Texan with a mean disposition, Ezell pitched and, in the words of one observer, "came very near knocking the stuffing out of three or four of the boys, and the boys swore they would not play with him."

Snowball fights always followed a winter storm, and they did much to break the tedium of camp life. These engage-

THIS PHOTOGRAPH FROM FORT PULASKI IS ONE OF THE FIRST SHOWING A BASEBALL GAME BEING PLAYED (IN BACKGROUND).

(NPS)

THE ROLE OF BLACK SOLDIERS

by James I. Robertson, Jr.

*J*ust as the black man played a central part in causing the Civil War, so did he play a major role in determining its outcome.

An Illinois soldier wrote of sentiments in 1861: "If the Negro was thought of at all, it was only as the firebrand that had caused the conflagration—the accursed that had created enmity and bitterness between the two sections, and excited the fratricidal strife." Quite in contrast was the observation of Pennsylvania soldier Oliver Norton. Writing from Virginia in January, 1862, Norton stated: "I thought I hated slavery as much as possible before I came here, but here, where I can see some of its workings, I am more than ever convinced of the cruelty and inhumanity of the system. It has not one redeeming feature."

The idea among Union officials of using former slaves as soldiers evolved slowly. It developed through stepping stones of hostility, discrimina-tion, and tragedy. Federal authorities had little objection to employing blacks as army laborers, but Northern senti-ment was widespread that arm-ing blacks would be degrading for the country. Others feared that mobilization would invite insurrection. Many Northerners agreed with Southern slave-holders: blacks were inferior beings incapable of fighting with the intensity and courage of white men.

Abolitionists, patriots, and humanitarians saw compelling reasons for placing blacks in uniform. Their numbers would add tremendous strength to Federal forces; their presence would give new meaning to the concept of American democra-cy; military service, from the blacks' point of view, would prepare and justify them for full admission into postwar society.

When Abraham Lincoln's Emancipation Proclamation went into effect on January 1, 1863, it opened the door for the formal recruitment of black sol-diers. Progress was slow because of reluctance on the part of large numbers of Union officials. Not until high-ranking Federal commanders under-went a change of attitude did the program gain momentum.

For example, in the summer of 1863, General U.S. Grant had seen enough to write Lincoln: "By arming the negro we have added a powerful ally. They will make good soldiers and taking them from the enemy weakens him in the same pro-portion they strengthen us. I am therefore most decidedly in favor of pushing this policy."

The most important fac-tor in the final acceptance of blacks as soldiers was their per-formance in battle. No amount of talk or propaganda could have won the black soldier a rightful place in the Union army. He had to achieve that place himself, soldier-fashion, in bloody combat. This they did, and proudly.

In the last half of the Civil War, black troops fought in 41 major battles and scores of minor engagements. At Port Hudson, La., on May 27, 1863, blacks made their first formal assault of the war. Some 1,080 of them were part of an attack against a 6,000-man Confederate garrison. The blacks did not flinch but literal-ly threw themselves against the enemy works. Over 300 blacks were listed among the casual-ties of the unsuccessful assault. Ten days later, at Milliken's

ATTACK ON FORT WAGNER BY THE 54TH MASSACHUSETTS, THE FIRST BLACK REGIMENT FROM THE NORTH TO GO TO WAR.

(LC)

Bend, La., the tables were reversed. Southerners assailed a position manned by black soldiers. Some of the most vicious fighting of the war ensued as the blacks held their lines.

Glory came to black soldiers the following month at Fort Wagner, S.C. Close to 5,000 Federals charged across a wide expanse of open beach against a strongly fortified position. In the forefront of the attack was the 54th Massachusetts, the first black regiment from the North to go to war. This unit had been struggling through tangled marshland for two days, in pouring rain and without food. Yet it surged forward heroically at Fort Wagner; in the illfated attack the blacks lost 100 killed, 145 wounded, and 100 captured. The *Atlantic Monthly* later declared: "Through the cannon smoke of that dark night, the manhood of the colored race shines before many eyes that would not see."

Throughout the Civil War, black soldiers had to weather a host of discriminations. The Confederacy initially refused to grant them the rights and privileges accorded to white Billy Yanks seized in battle. For most of their Civil War service, blacks received only half the pay of whites. They served in completely segregated regiments and, with rare exceptions, were led by white officers. The worst duties in camp and field customarily went to black commands. Their uniforms and equipment as often as not were discards and rejects.

Constant harassment from white Billy Yanks further hampered the efforts of the blacks to attain recognition. In the summer of 1861, an Indiana lieutenant wrote his sister: "I do not believe it right to make soldiers of them and class & rank them with our white soldiers.... I do despise them, and the more I see of them, the more I am against the whole black race." A New York soldier

once made the terse comment: "I think the best way to settle the question of what to do with the darkies would be to shoot them."

Many of those feelings never ameliorated, but the majority of them did. After the bloody 1864 battle of Nashville, Union General George H. Thomas looked at the battlefield strewn with bodies and exclaimed: "Gentlemen, the question is settled. Negroes will fight."

A total of about 179,000 blacks served as soldiers in the Civil War and later on the western frontier. They were organized into 120 infantry regiments, 22 artillery batteries, and 7 cavalry regiments. Cumulative losses in black units in the 1860s and 1870s were unusually high: 68,200—more than a third of the total enrolled. Of that number, 2,750 were killed in action; the remaining 65,450 perished from wounds and sickness. The number of desertions among black troops was about 7% of the total in the army. Twenty-one blacks received the Congressional Medal of Honor for gallantry in action.

In 1892, Colonel Norwood P. Hall of the 55th Massachusetts (Colored) Regiment proudly stated of his men: "We called upon them in the day of our trial, when volunteering had ceased, when the draft was a partial failure, and the bounty system a senseless extravagance. They were ineligible for promotion, they were not to be treated as prisoners of war. Nothing was definite except that they could be shot or hanged as soldiers. Fortunate it is for [the nation], as well as for them, that they were equal to the crisis; that the grand historic moment which comes to a race only once in many centuries came to them, and that they recognized it ..."

BLACK TROOPS LIBERATE SLAVES IN NORTH CAROLINA. WOODCUT FROM *HARPER'S WEEKLY*, JANUARY 1864.

(LC)

ments usually occurred among small groups, although they might involve large numbers of men. One such contest erupted between the 2nd and the 12th New Hampshire. In the action, wrote one bystander, "tents were wrecked, bones broken, eyes blacked, and teeth knocked out—all in fun."

An Iowa soldier, writing to his father in 1863, philosophized: "There is one thing certain, the Army will either make a man better or worse morally speaking." This Midwesterner was pessimistic in the overall picture of soldier conduct. "There is no mistake but the majority of soldiers are a hard lot. It would be hard for you to imagine worse than they are. They have every temptation to do wrong and if a man has not firmness enough to keep from the excesses common to soldiers he will soon be as bad as the worst."

PLAYING CARDS KEPT THE TROOPS OCCUPIED.
(COURTESY SPECIAL COLLECTIONS, EMORY UNIVERSITY)

MEN OF COMPANY B, 170TH NEW YORK INFANTRY, RELAX IN THE FIELD BY PLAYING CARDS AND CHECKERS OR READING.
(LC)

night at any camp. As for profanity, a Billy Yank observed of his first encampment: "There is so much swearing in this place it would set anyone against that if from no other motive but disgust at hearing it." Army life of the 1860s—with all of its inadequacies and hardships—lent itself to men venting frustrations in salty language. Few had any hesitation in doing so.

Every army in the Civil War contained some degree of lawlessness. Theft was the most common offense. It was often stated that no farmer's henhouse was safe when the 21st Illinois was encamped in the vicinity. The 6th New York also acquired an unsavory reputation.

Gambling and profanity were natural by-products of camp life. Dominoes, checkers, and chess were well-liked diversions, but they were not in the same class with card games. Poker, twenty-one, euchre, and keno were in evidence any

One officer described this New York City unit as "the very flower of the Dead Rabbits, creme de la creme of Bowery society." Rumor circulated that before a man was accepted in the 6th New York, he had to prove that he possessed a jail record.

Just before that particular unit departed for war, its colonel gave the men a pep talk. He held up his gold watch and proclaimed that Southern plantation owners all had such luxuries which awaited confiscation by Union soldiers. Five minutes later, the colonel reached in his pocket to check on the time and found his watch gone.

The pronounced individualism of American generations during that era explains in great part the disrespect for authority so commonplace in the armies. Southerners and Northerners who answered the call to arms were products of a new nation dedicated to the ideal that one man was as good as another; and when many of the officers showed themselves to be at least as inexperienced as the men they were supposed to be leading, soldiers in the ranks reacted in disgust.

These were civilian armies, formed hastily by the first fires of war. Most of the men in a company had been lifelong acquaintances. Before entering the army, they had addressed one another as John, Tom, or Harry; but once in military service, several of their friends became their superior officers. Men who had never so much as doffed their hats at one another now found themselves obligated to salute each other and to obey orders without question. Relinquishing friendly informality for stuffy formality taxed the tempers of more than one private.

A North Carolinian pointedly explained the situation in his company: "The rank and file of the Anson Guards

AN UNIDENTIFIED OFFICER (LEFT) POSES WITH AN ENLISTED MAN.

(COURTESY OF DENNIS KEESEE)

were the equals, and superiors to some of their officers; socially, in wealth, in position and in education, and it was a hard lesson to learn respectful obedience." In other words, the average soldier was willing to obey all orders that were sensible, provided the man giving them did not get too puffed up about it.

Verbal attacks on officers were frequent and involved the use of such references as "whorehouse pimp," "a vain, stuck-up, illiterate ass," "a whining methodist class leader," and one of the most classic of all time: "a God damned fussy old pisspot." Yet the phrase that got the most men hauled before a

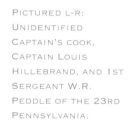

PICTURED L-R: UNIDENTIFIED CAPTAIN'S COOK, CAPTAIN LOUIS HILLEBRAND, AND 1ST SERGEANT W.R. PEDDLE OF THE 23RD PENNSYLVANIA.

(USAMHI)

military court was the time-honored "son of a bitch."

A Southerner once classified his colonel as "an ignoramus fit for nothing higher than the cultivation of corn." One soldier from Florida was convinced that all officers were "not fit to tote guts to a bear." Billy Yanks shared such feelings. "The officers," one Massachusetts soldier asserted, "consider themselves as made of a different material from the low fellows in the ranks. . . . They get all the glory and most of the pay and don't earn ten cents apiece on the dollar the drunken rascals."

When a thoroughly disliked general succumbed to illness early in 1865, one of his men wrote home: "Old Landers is ded. . . . I did not see a tear shed but heard a great many speaches made about him such as he was in hell pumping thunder at 3 cents a clap." Yet the choicest denunciation of all came from an Illinois private who once intoned: "I wish to God one half of our officers were knocked in the head by slinging them Against A part of those still Left."

In contrast, those officers who led with gentle persuasiveness and possessed real understanding about their men almost without exception received obedience and respect. When widely esteemed Colonel Edward E. Cross of the 5th New Hampshire fell mortally wounded at Gettysburg, his last words were: "I think the boys will miss me." They did; the regiment was never quite the same after Cross's death.

Alcohol consumption triggered the most continual misbehavior in Civil War camps. The men drank for several reasons

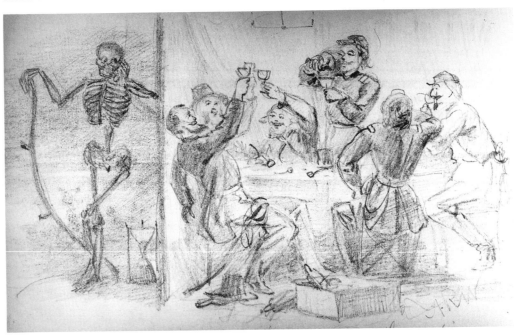

and usually to excess. A Louisianian stated of a compatriot: "I never knew before that Clarence was so much addicted to drinking. If he had been as fond of his mother's milk, as he is of whiskey, he would have been awful hard to wean."

Most of the whiskey brought or smuggled into the armies could be classified as "mean" even for that day. A Hoosier soldier analyzed one issue of whiskey and with a straight face adjudged it to be a combination of "bark juice, tar-water, turpentine, brown sugar, lamp-oil and alcohol." The potency of the liquor is readily evident from some of the nicknames given to it: "Old Red Eye," "Rifle Knock-Knee," "How Come You So," and "Help Me to Sleep, Mother."

The liquid surely produced some startling reactions, especially among commanders. One night in the spring of 1861, Confederate General Arnold Elzey and his staff engaged in a long and boisterous party. Whiskey flowed copiously. At one point, a fairly inebriated Elzey called in the sentry guarding his tent and kindly gave the man a drink. The revelry eventually ran its course; Elzey collapsed in bed and fell into a deep sleep. About dawn, he was aroused by the sentinel, who exclaimed: "General! General! Ain't it about time for us to take another drink?"

In February 1864, the officers of the 126th Ohio had a farewell party for their colonel. A bucket each of egg nog and bourbon came into play. The result, according to a disgusted bystander, "was a big drunk, and such a weaving, spewing, sick set of men I have not seen for many a day . . . Col. Harlan was dead drunk. One Capt. who is a Presbyterian elder at home was not much better."

The 48th New York, commanded by the Reverend James M. Perry, was such a model of good behavior that the regiment became known as "Perry's Saints." However, while the men were stationed at Tybee Island, Georgia, in 1862, a large cargo of beer and wine washed ashore after a storm. The New Yorkers proceeded to get wildly intoxicated. This spree may have been a leading factor in Colonel Perry suffering a fatal heart attack at his desk the following day.

On another occasion, an inebriated Union corps commander walked straight into a tree in front of his tent, then had to be restrained from arresting the officer of the guard on charges of felonious assault.

Army punishments were imperative for the survival of discipline. Yet the lead-

ing characteristics of Civil War punishments were inequity and capriciousness. The frequency and degree of army sentences depended in large measure on the whims of the commanding officer. Sometimes the most serious offenses were all but ignored, while on other occasions trifling offenses resulted in severe punishments.

Drunken soldiers tied up for fighting and other unruly conduct.

Most penalties meted out in the army were exhibitionistic. Marching through camp with signs denoting "Thief" or "Coward" were common punishments. Other penalties included having to wear a barrel shirt, dragging a ball and chain, and a painful punishment called "bucking and gagging." After seeing a man sentenced to the last-named humiliation, a soldier described his plight. "A bayonette or piece of wood was placed in his mouth and a string tied behind his ears kept it in position"; then "the man was seated on the ground with his knees drawn up to his body. A piece of wood is run through his legs, and placing his arms under the stick on each side of his knees, his hands are then tied in front, and he is as secure as a trapped rat." In this posture, the culprit would undergo excruciating pain for several hours.

Long jail terms, branding, and dishonorable discharges were punishments generally reserved for deserters, flagrant cowards, or men repeatedly guilty of insubordination. Far more frequently than might be imagined was the use of capital punishment. Some 500 Civil War soldiers went before firing squads or mounted crudely constructed gallows. Two-thirds of that number met their deaths because of the single crime of desertion. Executions were not merely public; they were usually mandatory in the case of the condemned man's brigade or division. Soldiers watching one of their number put to death for a serious offense were not likely to commit the same offense, the thinking went.

A COWARD IS DRUMMED
FROM THE RANKS OF
THE ARMY OF THE
POTOMAC.
ILLUSTRATION FROM
HARPER'S WEEKLY,
1862.

Food was the worst problem in all Civil War armies. It produced the most criticisms of army life. Apparently the thinking on both sides was that if the government supplied the basic foodstuffs to the men in large enough proportions, the troops would make out satisfactorily. Such thinking worked out well in camp; but when the

Pennsylvania soldier John H. Markley observed in 1863 that his salted beef ration "was so strong it could almost walk itself." An Illinois infantryman examined the meat he received on one occasion and declared that "one can throw a piece up against a tree and it will just stick there and quiver and twitch for all the world like one of those blue-bellied lizards at home will do when you knock him off a fence rail with a stick."

The standard bread ration in the Union armies was a three-inch-square cracker known as hardtack. It was shipped southward in large crates

FORBES DRAWING
"FALL IN FOR SOUP."

(LC)

armies were on the move, food was almost always scarce. Every regiment in the field experienced at least one food shortage in the course of the war, while in some military theaters famines of lengthy duration took place.

As a rule, the rations varied from mediocre to downright repugnant. In the autumn of 1862 an Illinois corporal informed the home folk: "The boys say our 'grub' is enough to make a mule desert, and a hog wish he had never been born. . . . Hard bread, bacon and coffee is all we draw."

Meat was always in short supply—and that may have been good fortune. Beef was distributed either fresh or pickled with salt. When chewable, the fresh meat was often eaten raw because it seemed to have more taste than when cooked.

marked "B. C.," denoting Brigade Commissary. Given the toughness of the crackers, Billy Yanks were convinced that the letters actually stood for the date when they were baked. Worse, shipments of these crackers were usually so infiltrated with "wigglies" that the most prevalent nickname given to hardtack was "worm castles." One soldier (perhaps with a degree of exaggeration) stated after the war: "All the fresh meat we had came in the hard bread . . . and I preferring my game cooked, used to toast my biscuits."

Civil War soldiers had wonderful powers of adaptation, but most of them never acclimat-

PRISONERS OF WAR

by James I. Robertson, Jr.

Fear of being captured scarcely entered the minds of Northern and Southern recruits who entered the armies. Americans had never faced the problem of significant numbers of prisoners of war. In past conflicts, those comparatively few enemy troops taken prisoner received battlefield paroles and generally vanished from the scene. However, the immense scope of the Civil War broke all traditions with the past. About 410,000 soldiers fell into the hands of the other side. This figure is 4-5 times greater than

the number of American soldiers captured in all of the nation's other wars combined.

Neither side had any knowledge of what to do with growing numbers of prisoners. An attempt at an exchange policy, begun in 1862, collapsed ingloriously the next year. In the course of the war, both sides were guilty of neglect and

mismanagement resulting in unnecessary suffering and needless deaths.

Sickness reigned in every one of the 20 to 25 major compounds of the war. (In all, over 150 prisons came into existence.) A Confederate surgeon, after inspecting one facility, filed a report that easily could have applied to any soldier prison. "From the crowded conditions, filthy habits, bad diet and dejected, depressed condition of the prisoners, their system had become so disordered that the smallest abrasion of the skin, from the rubbing of a shoe, or from the effects of the sun, the prick of a splinter or the scratching of a mosquito bite,

in some cases took on a rapid and frightful ulceration and gangrene."

Soldiers unlucky enough to be captured usually went first to a depot compound such as Point Lookout, Maryland, or Libby Prison in Richmond. From there most captives were transferred to the prisons that would be their

homes for the remainder of the war.

Prominent Northern prisons were Fort Warren, Mass.; Elmira, N.Y.; Old Capitol, D.C.; Fort Delaware, Del.; Camp Douglas and Rock Island, Ill.; and Johnson's Island, Ohio. In the South the major prisons were at Richmond and Danville, Va.; Salisbury, N.C.; Columbia and Charleston, S.C.; Andersonville, Ga.; and Camp Ford, Texas.

Prison routine was painfully monotonous. Soldiers arose at dawn, answered roll call, and received some kind of rations. A second meal came in the afternoon, with another roll call at sundown. During the remaining 23 hours of each day, prisoners were left to their thoughts and improvisations.

Because Andersonville was the largest of the Civil War prisons, it has received the most attention from generations of writers. It had a record that remains vile by any standard. The compound was hastily laid out late in the war and designed for 10,000 prisoners. At one point, more than 33,000 Federals were crammed into the open and barren expanse. Most of the captives sent there were "old fish," prisoners sent from other compounds. Andersonville held a total of 49,400 prisoners during its 13-month existence. Over 13,700 of those men perished from overcrowding, malnutrition, and insufficient medical care.

Closely matching Andersonville's death rate, on a smaller scale, was the Union prison camp at Elmira, New York. Of 12,147 Confederates held there, 2,980 succumbed from the same causes present at Andersonville.

Each side accused the other of atrocity, cruelty, and barbarism, yet neither North nor South made any concerted endeavor to improve conditions.

As one would expect, soldiers' opinions of prison life were consistently negative. Inmates referred to various

MANY UNION PRISONERS OF WAR WERE HELD AT LIBBY PRISON IN RICHMOND, VA.

(LC)

prison administrators as "the little snotty dog," an "Ass of a Lieut." and "a most savage looking man," "a vulgar, coarse brute," and "the greatest scoundrel that ever went unhung." Speaking of a trio of officials at Fort Delaware, a Tennessee prisoner asserted: "I Dont Think Thar is any Place in Hell Hot anuf for Thos 3 men."

In the case of the guards at Andersonville, a Federal prisoner stated that "we are under the Malishia & their ages range from 10 to 75 & they are the Dambst set of men I ever had the Luck to fall in with yet."

Rations issued to Federal officer-prisoners at Libby, a New Englander stated, "consisted of about twenty-two ounces of bread and thirty ounces of meat for each week. We had something else that they gave us one week; I do not know what the name of it was." A Confederate at Camp Douglas in Chicago was explicit about some meat he received: a hunk of mule neck with the hair still attached.

No doubt exists but that all prisoners fought a constant battle against vermin. A New York officer found fleas to be particularly obnoxious. "The beasts crawled over the ground from body to body, and their attacks seemed to become more aggravating as the men became more emaciated. By daylight, they could be picked off . . . but in the darkness there was nothing to do but suffer with patience."

Literally hundreds of "memoirs" by former prisoners of war appeared in print after the Civil War. The authenticity and accuracy of the majority have always been in question. Each former prisoner who picked up pen and paper seemed to feel duty bound to present a more horrible picture of conditions than did the last writer. These accounts in most instances were propagandistic and political; they fed the flames of a controversy that rages still.

Of the 215,000 Johnny Rebs and 195,000 Billy Yanks taken prisoner in the Civil War, 56,000 died in confinement. The prison death rate is less than that of most military hospitals at the time. Yet so many of those incarcerated soldiers lost their lives through incompetence and indifference that beclouds the whole prison subject with deep sadness.

George F. Root's "Tramp! Tramp! Tramp!" was one of the best-known war songs of the 1860s because it was written from the viewpoint of a prisoner of war whose feelings mirrored those of the captured men of both sides. The opening lines are:

In the prison cell I sit, thinking,
Mother dear, of you,

And our bright and happy
house so far away.

And the tears they fill my eyes,
spite of all that I can do,

Tho' I try to cheer my comrades
and be gay.

ed to the quality and quantity of Civil War rations. One thoroughly disgusted private spoke for the majority when he informed his brother: "We live so mean here. the hard bread is all worms and the meat stinks like hell . . . and rice two or three times a week & worms as long as your finger. I liked rice once but god dam the stuff now."

Despite such complaints, hunger was a regular companion to several Union armies and to all Confederate forces in the field. The problem was not in supply, for both sides had strong agricultural bases. Transportation breakdowns, graft, corrup-

tion, and bureaucratic incompetence blocked tons of foodstuffs from reaching the front lines. Soldiers therefore resorted to extreme measures in an effort to calm the gnawing emptiness in their stomachs.

Some troops were known to subsist for days on green apples and unripe peaches taken from orchards alongside the route of a march. A South Carolina colonel stated after the war that he "frequently saw the hungry Confederates gather up the dirt and corn where a horse had been fed, so that when he reached his bivouac he could wash out the dirt and gather the few grains of corn to satisfy in part at least the cravings of hunger. Hard, dry, parched corn . . . was for many days the sole diet of all."

A Virginian once boiled his greasy haversack in an attempt to make soup. In 1864 a South Carolina private, overcome by what he termed his "bold and aggressive appetite," confessed that he had "devoured the hindquarters of a muskrat with vindictive relish, and looked with longing eyes upon our adjutant-general's pointer dog."

Sickness and insufficient medical treatment were the worst enemies that Johnny Rebs and Billy Yanks faced.

Midway through the Civil War a Southern private swore that he "had rather face the Yankees than the sickness and there is always more men dies of sickness than in battle." This soldier was tragically correct. For every man killed in action during the Civil War, two died behind the lines of illness and disease. Extant records show over 6,000,000 reported cases of sickness in the Union armies alone. Surgeon Joseph Jones tabulated that every Confederate soldier was ill an average of six times in the course of the war.

Several factors, each with major impact, accounted for the high incidence of sickness. The ease with which a man could enter the army in the first half of the war, the poor condition of many of the recruits, and the abysmal camp conditions were the first causes. Encampment sites were selected primarily for military reasons and rarely for health considerations. Such locations tended to be used repeatedly. Inadequate drainage, ignorance of sanitation practices, plus the natural carelessness of life in camp added to the setting for widespread illness. Exposure to the elements, general filth, improper diet, and always-present vermin compounded the situation. A woeful lack of medical knowledge, critical shortage of army surgeons, and total inexperience in dealing with both traumatic injuries and large numbers of incapacitated soldiers further intensified four years of human suffering. Only hints at that time existed that unseeable objects called germs played any part in

sickness or infection. That flies and mosquitoes might be carriers of disease was widely regarded as preposterous.

Before they heard their first hostile shots, the soldiers encountered two onslaughts of illness. First were the so-called "childhood diseases" that struck the farmboys and others who had accumulated no immunities. Chicken pox, measles, mumps, and whooping cough plowed through new regiments in epidemic pro-

portions. Measles was the deadliest of these diseases. An Iowa soldier visited a warehouse where one batch of measles cases had been deposited. "About 100 sick men crowded into a room 60 by 100 feet in all stages of measles. The poor boys lying on the hard floor, with only one or two blankets under them, not even straw, and anything they could find for a pillow. Many sick and vomiting, many already showing unmistakable signs of blood poisoning."

While the troops struggled helplessly against the first wave of diseases, they also had to endure "camp illnesses" triggered by impure water, exposure, poor food, mosquitoes, and general filth. Such conditions

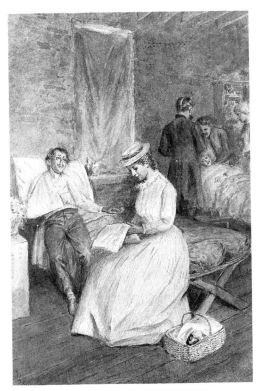

Most Civil War soldiers were unaware of the severe handicaps under which the doctors labored, especially during a battle. In the rude and makeshift field hospitals only a mile or two behind the battle lines, physicians toiled long hours to rescue life from the debris of war. Field surgeons performed three basic tasks only. They probed for embedded missiles (usually with their fingers), and they employed unsophisticated ligatures in an effort to control hemorrhaging. However, three-fourths of a surgeon's time was spent in amputating mangled arms and legs. Little was known at the time of the principle of setting broken bones; of greater impact was the simple rationale that the wounded were too

produced the biggest killers of the Civil War: diarrhea, dysentery, typhoid fever, and pneumonia.

Diarrhea was practically a universal epidemic among Civil War soldiers. It was at the least debilitating and at the most deadly. Army physicians were never able to find any suitable cure or even to provide a semblance of relief. This led an Illinois soldier to remark on one occasion that a compatriot's bowels "needs turning ron side out and washing with soap suds." After the war an Iowa soldier noted humorously that countless numbers of men "literally had no stomach for fighting."

Medical knowledge was at such a primitive stage in the 1860s that the practice of army medicine devolved into administering drugs and potions of all known types and in heavy quantities. One New England surgeon habitually plied men suffering from any ailment (including diarrhea) with dose after dose of castor oil. As he did so, he would state cheerily: "Down with it, my boy. The more you take, the less I carry."

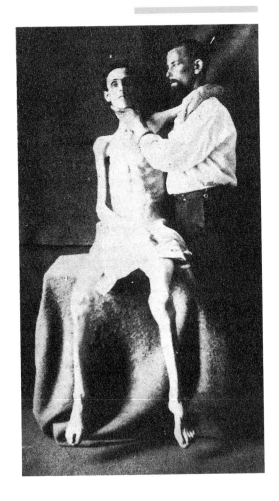

many and the doctors too few to allow prolonged treatment of a serious injury to an extremity. It was quicker, and the prognosis seemed just as favorable, to remove the limb in question.

Any soldier who saw a field hospital never forgot it. At the first major battle of the war, Lieutenant William Blackford and his Virginia cavalry company patrolled one of the vital roads. It was early in the afternoon when Blackford observed that "along a shady little valley through which our road lay the surgeons had been plying their vocation all the morning upon the wounded. Tables about breast high had been erected upon which screaming victims were having legs and arms cut off. The surgeons and their assistants, stripped to the waist and all bespattered with blood, stood around, some holding the poor fellows while others, armed with long bloody knives and saws, cut and sawed away with frightful rapidity, throwing the mangled limbs on a pile near by as soon as removed. Many were stretched on the ground awaiting their turn, many more were arriving continually . . . while those upon whom operations had already been performed calmly fanned the flies from their wounds. The battle roared in front . . . but the prayers, the curses, the screams, the blood, the flies, the sickening stench of this horrible little valley were too much for the stomachs of the men, and all along the column, leaning over the pommels of their saddles, they could be seen in ecstasies of protest."

Army surgeons were not miracle men: they lacked both the knowledge and the medications to curb epidemics, to stop the spread of infection, and to restore health to every man who was ailing. Hence, they were incompetent in the eyes of many sick soldiers. "Because a man had enlisted to serve his country," an artilleryman asserted, "it is no reason he should be treated like a dog by one-horse country doctors who once they mount shoulder straps, think they are Almighty." A Midwestern private worked up what he regarded as the supreme criticism when he stated that "the docterking [was] about in keeping [with] the Cooking."

The surgeons labored on as best they could in the face of such damnation. One Confederate physician put the subject in perspective (at least to his own satisfaction) when he concluded: "Medical Officers are generally the most unpopular—owing to the fact that they deal with sick men—the most unreasonable of all animals."

As for those soldiers outspoken in their denunciation of surgeons, few of them would have considered Dr. George T. Stevens of the 76th New York pausing in the midst of the 1864 Wilderness campaign in Virginia to inform his wife: "I see so many grand men dropping one by one. They are acquaintances and my friends. They look to me for help, and I have to turn away heartsick at my want of ability to relieve their

It is a shocking fact that at least a third of the Southern army was barefoot at any given time. Commanders worried constantly about the men suffering from want of shoes, particularly in wintertime. One Confederate brigadier sought to alleviate the situation by issuing strips of fresh cowhide to his men to wrap around their feet. The result of using untreated hide was disastrous, according to one Johnny Reb. "General Armstad sent me a pair of raw hide shoes the other day and [they] stretch out at the heel so that when I start down a hill they whip me nearly to death. they flop up and down. they stink very bad and I have to keep a bush in my hand to keep the flies off of them." However, the soldier added, "this is the last of the raw hide, for some of the boys got hungry last

sufferings. . . . Oh! can I ever write anything besides these mournful details? Hundreds of ambulances are coming into town now, and it is almost midnight. So they come every night."

Lack of adequate clothing brought misery and suffering to thousands of soldiers. Men in the Union Army of the Potomac likened the winter of 1862-1863 around Fredericksburg, Virginia, to the agony of George Washington's army at Valley Forge. A member of the 13th New Hampshire observed: "It is fearful to wake at night, and to hear the sounds made by the men around you. All night long the sounds go up of men coughing, moaning and groaning with acute pain. . . . This camp of 100,000 men is practically a vast hospital."

night and boiled them and ate them, so farewell raw hide shoes."

Unhealthy camp conditions were commonplace. Little opportunity existed for bathing. Since most soldiers had but one uniform, it appeared a waste of time to wash oneself in a river and then don the same filthy rags again. Confederate soldiers suffered harshly in this regard. Following the 1862 battle of Antietam, Lieutenant James Burnham of Connecticut told his parents of seeing Confederate prisoners of war for the first time. "Their hair was long and uncombed and their faces were thin and cadaverous as though they had been starved to death. It is of course possible that it is the natural look of the race, but it appeared mightily to me like the result of short fare. They were the dirtiest set I ever beheld. A regiment of New England paupers could not equal them for the filth, lice and rags."

The use and misuse of camp latrines—long, open ditches with no sanitary aspects whatsoever—further promoted germs and disease. Many soldiers scorned the foul-smelling "sinks," as latrines were called. Thus did a Virginia soldier write in his diary in 1862: "On rolling up my bed this morning I found I had been lying in—I wont say what—something though that didn't smell like milk and peaches."

A contaminated atmosphere where tens of thousands of unwashed soldiers

congregated led to an endless horde of flies, mosquitoes, gnats, lice, and fleas, which themselves became additional hazards to health. "There are more flies here than I ever saw any where before," an Alabama volunteer wrote his wife. "Sometimes I . . . commence killing them but as I believe forty come to everyone's funeral I have given it up as a bad job."

Few soldiers escaped infestation by fleas. A Mississippi soldier, returning to camp from a short furlough, wrote about the onslaught of fleas he encountered. "They hav most Eate me up since I came

Back her," he declared. "I was fresh to them so they pitched in." Fleas likewise plagued an Alabama private and led to an interesting commentary by that man to his wife: "I think there are 50 on my person at this time, but you know they never did trouble me. . . . May, I have thought of you often while mashing fleas."

Vermin swarmed wherever an army assembled. Battle was no deterrent. A Federal colonel once waved his men into action with a sword in one hand while he feverishly scratched himself with the other hand.

Civil War soldiers took varying degrees of refuge in religion. For most troops, religion was a personal matter. Joining the army only strengthened their conviction to follow home-learned Christian principles down the uncertain road of war. Hence, faith in God became

the single greatest instrument in the maintenance of morale inside the armies. The evangelical sects of the nineteenth century were active and large. From the writings of Johnny Rebs and Billy Yanks comes the inescapable conclusion that faith was more prevalent in the ranks than is the case in modern times.

A few men, of course, dismissed religion as a weakness or scorned faith after witnessing the hell of battle or experiencing the loss of friends and comrades. Some soldiers just grew weary of the loud evangelicalism present in camp. Among the latter was Sergeant James Williams of the 21st Alabama.

After having to endure the noise of yet another nightly camp meeting, Williams sneered: "It seems to me that where ever I go I can never get rid of the Psalm-singers . . . making night hideous with their horrid nasal twang butchering bad music, and insulting the Most High with hypocritical and 'impious prayers!'" Williams had no confidence either in the fighting qualities of the openly devout. "If I had to go off on a dangerous expedition to-night, I'd rather take an old granny than any of them—Give me a good 'sinner' to stand by me when the hour of danger comes."

Far larger numbers of soldiers found in religion a sanctuary from war and all of its uncertainties. One such Confederate, James Parrott of the 16th Tennessee, reassured his wife: "I can say thank God that I have never bin harmed. when I go into a fite I say God be my helper and when I come out I say thank God I feel like he has bin with mee."

Reading testaments was a common occurrence in camp. Chaplains usually spoke to large and attentive audiences at a field service. Religious tracts found eager takers whenever they were circulated. Many soldiers, unsure of the unknowns of tomorrow, seconded the sentiments of Abraham Lincoln, who once acknowledged: "I have often been driven to my knees by the realization that I had nowhere else to go."

The personal religion of Johnny Rebs and Billy Yanks manifested itself in intimate and sometimes interesting prayers. Just before the start of one large battle, a group of North Carolinians asked a compatriot who was also a self-styled preacher to lead them in prayer. The man removed his hat, looked heavenward, and intoned:

"Lord, if you ain't with us, don't be agin us. Just step aside

Southern chaplains "a race of loud-mouthed ranters . . . offensively loquacious upon every topic of life save man's salvation." A hospital chaplain made a habit of sitting on the edge of some soldier's cot, telling the man he looked close to death, and urging him to prepare to meet his Maker. This was too much for one recuperating soldier; he threw a plate at the cleric and told him to go to hell.

Lack of scruples characterized a number of early army ministers. Court-martial records show that some descended to horse-stealing, speculation, theft, and desertion. One rainy evening, a chaplain entered a stud-poker game in the camp of a Connecticut unit and

and watch the damndest fight you are ever likely to see!"

The bulwarks of faith in the armies were supposed to be the chaplains. Yet evidence is strong that many of the initial appointees did not practice what they preached. An Englishman serving in the Confederate army termed the first group of

promptly cleaned out an entire company.

Such behavior brought momentary discredit to the whole profession and a variety of nicknames to individual offenders. One chaplain remembered only for hellfire-and-brimstone sermons was dubbed "The Great Thunderer"; another who continually warned soldiers of imminent death was called "Death on a Pale Horse"; and when the chaplain of the 127th New York began charging the troops a penny apiece for each letter he mailed home for them, the soldiers contemptuously christened him "One Cent by God."

Fortunately, these incompetents eventually left the armies.

The men who remained—known affectionately as "Holy Joe" or "Holy John"—proved to be sincerely motivated, unpretentious, filled with both righteousness and patriotism, and able to bring a sense of caring in an aura of callous warfare. The good chaplains performed a wide variety of activities: holding prayer meetings and church services on a regular basis, visiting the sick in camp and hospital, counseling with individual soldiers, distributing religious tracts and testaments, writing and reading letters for soldiers, delivering mail, enduring the hardships of their men on the march and in battle, and making of themselves an example for the troops to follow. Chaplains were generally judged far

more for what they did than for what they said; and if they turned out to be good preachers as well, that was an extra point in their favor.

The kindness of chaplains to soldiers was never forgotten. On a particularly trying march in 1863, Chaplain William E. Wiatt of the 26th Virginia carried the guns of several weakened men in his regiment. This exertion so sapped the Baptist cleric that he was confined to bed for a week. Yet Wiatt's actions won him scores of lifelong friends.

Another example was the Reverend Arthur Fuller of the 16th Massachusetts. He fell at Fredericksburg, Virginia, musket in hand, while participating in a skirmish. Two days earlier, Fuller had received his discharge from service. He had delayed his departure to remain with his friends a little longer. Similarly, Mississippi Chaplain A. G. Burrows returned to camp with the troops after a skirmish with Federals. Burrows had a four-inch gash in his skull. "It was winter and bitter cold," a fellow minister noted. "The wounded chaplain had no overcoat.

The kindness of chaplains to soldiers was never forgotten. On a particularly trying march in 1863, Chaplain William E. Wiatt of the 26th Virginia carried the guns of several weakened men in his regiment.

A GROUP OF CONFEDERATE SOLDIERS POSE FOR A WAR PHOTOGRAPHER.

(LC)

39

THE HOME FIRES

by William Marvel

The Civil War was waged not only on the battlefields and in the camps, but well behind the lines. From the New England farmer who hired a boy in place of his soldier son, to the Piedmont housewife who roasted chicory root as a substitute for her family's coffee, American civilians could not ignore the conflict.

The South obviously bore the brunt of civilian sacrifice and suffering. Even by the final months of 1861, before Federal armies had struck deeply into Confederate territory, the naval blockade had begun to whittle away at the Southern standard of living. Culinary delicacies and creature comforts quickly became scarce (and thus more expensive) for a society that had long imported most of its goods. As the war progressed, drugs and other medical supplies disappeared. Salt, which proved so essential to food preservation and the curing of animal hides, became the foremost commodity on the black market. Field armies absorbed all that Confederate industry could produce. A higher proportion of Southern farmers died or came home disabled than their Northern counterparts, and a greater percentage were taken for the army; as the remaining growers turned to speculation in cotton and other cash crops, shortages developed even among the staple foods that the agrarian South had traditionally provided for itself.

While an early lack of fine wines or dress silk afflicted only the upper classes, the resulting increase of prices struck more painfully with each step down the social ladder. Poorer Southerners suffered more, however, from the plummeting value of Confederate paper currency. Inflation spiraled in triple digits through most of the war,

and by the middle of the conflict the Confederate capital was the scene of a bread riot. Decline in the production of food, a dearth of salt, and the destruction of stores and transportation by the Union armies brought some regions to the brink of famine by the end of 1864, dragging thousands of deserters out of the fight and shattering the will of many Southerners to continue the struggle.

Nearly every Northern community escaped outright want. Money, and to some extent manpower, composed the principal difficulties for civilians in the loyal states. Government contracts increased job opportunities but did not always improve the worker's economic situation. Often, wartime production meant longer hours and lower pay: even as carpenters at the Portsmouth naval shipyard finished the sloop that would sink the Confederate cruiser *Alabama*, the commandant announced that the workday would begin thereafter at sunrise, and wages would be cut by as much as one-quarter.

Although inflation posed a less serious problem for U.S. citizens than it did in the Confederacy, it still ate away at the workingman's ability to support himself, and the introduction of large numbers of women into the unskilled work force helped to diminish the labor demands that might have swelled wages enough to offset the shrinking value of greenbacks. Industry did lose a substantial ratio of its skilled workers to the army and navy, but New England agriculture probably felt the greatest labor shortage. For two decades New England farm families had been losing their sons to manufacturing or to the more fertile soil of

the plains; geography did not adapt the rocky Yankee hill farms to the mechanical implements that supplemented scarce labor north of the Ohio, and the sudden exodus of thousands of prime farm hands forced many New Englanders to reduce crops drastically. Many such farms never resumed their former production, and the war at least accelerated the decline of agriculture in the Northeast.

Rich or poor, the male Northern citizen preoccupied himself at one time or another with the possibility that he might be drafted, but most never saw an armed rebel or endured any fear of enemy depredations against himself or his property. Even during the great raids into Maryland and Pennsylvania, Confederates did not pillage the countryside, taking only horses and provisions with little wanton destruction, whereas Southerners whose homes lay in the path of Union armies frequently lost everything they owned and occasionally suffered personal violence as well. The difference lay in the military philosophies of the contending sides. Southern forces operated largely to defeat or discourage the Union armies, after the genteel European fashion; Federal generals like William Sherman eventually realized that the swiftest path to victory was to destroy the very fabric of Southern society, striking simultaneously at the Confederacy's military might and civilian morale.

A WOODCUT DEPICTING THE DISTRIBUTION OF RATIONS.

(LC)

myself if I were to meet up with one, though I recon I would learn before I left her."

Prostitution thrived during the war years. From a Kentucky encampment in the spring of 1864, an Indiana soldier wrote his family in disgust: "The godlessness [of this area] is great, cursing and whoring cries to heavn. Men from our company, yes even married ones, have gone to whore houses and paid 5 and 6 dollars per night. I was astonished. If their wives would know about it, it would cause terrific fights and maybe divorce. That's why I don't want to name them."

His other coat was thin and ragged. All his clothing was worn out." Burrows died shortly thereafter, "his devotion to his God and his country" having "cost him his life."

Two great revivals swept through the Confederate armies in the course of the war, and lesser religious awakenings marked other armies at some point. These movements doubtless elevated faith as well as morality. Yet evidence is strong that such improvements too often were temporary. Evil seems to have remained just as persistent in an army camp as the crusade for righteousness.

Nostalgia is always the great enemy of soldier morale. This was especially true of the men of blue and gray, most of whom were away from home for the first time. Moreover, these were young men looking for excitement and susceptible to temptations. As a Virginian told his cousin: "I have not seen a gal in so long a time that I would not know what to do with

In 1863, more than 7,000 prostitutes were working in Washington, D.C. Some of the bordellos in the Northern capital had such stimulating names as "The Haystack," "Hooker's Headquarters," and "Madame

Russell's Bake Oven." Richmond, Virginia, the capital of the Confederacy, was hardly any better. One madam there opened a bawdy house immediately across the street from a soldier hospital. Shortly thereafter, the hospital superintendent complained angrily that the prognosis of many of his patients had taken sharp turns for the worse. Prostitutes, he explained, were appearing at their windows in various stages of nudity, and they were making highly provocative gestures. As a result, patients were sneaking and hobbling from the hospital with little thought to the seriousness of their condition.

More often than not, soldiers North and South displayed the rude strength of youth by exhibiting a terrible capacity for loneliness. Two months into the war, Captain Harley Wayne of an Illinois regiment wrote his wife that many of his lads were grieving with homesickness. "I found one crying this morning," Wayne reported. "I tried to comfort him but had hard work to keep from joining him."

Accentuating that loneliness was a sentimentality deep and characteristic of the 1860s. The Civil War brought those two emotions together and created a deep love alien to most modern generations caught in the whirlpool of life in the late twentieth century. Romance was an overpowering sentiment among the men of blue and gray.

Once in the army, acquiring a sweetheart became a triumph just short of victory in battle. Illinois soldier John Shank wrote home about his new girlfriend: "I intend to have her for my wedded wife if I ever get home safe again. She is about 16 years old. She has black eyes and dark hair and fair skin and plenty of land and that aint all." Another Billy Yank was more specific about his new love. "My girl is none of

your one horse girls," he announced. "She is a regular stub and twister. She is well-educated and refined, all wildcat and fur, and Union from the muzzle to the crupper."

HEADQUARTERS OF HOOD'S TEXAS BRIGADE IN VIRGINIA.

(MC)

Soldiers and the folks back home generally maintained the most regular correspondence possible. Georgia soldier William Stillwell was a great tease; he enjoyed bantering with the home folk, and one suspects that he did so in great part to bolster the morale of all concerned. Stillwell had not seen his wife for a year when he informed her in matter-of-fact terms: "If I did not write and receive letters from you I believe that I would forgit that I was marrid. I dont feel much like a maryed man but I never forgit it sofar as to court enny other lady, but if I should you must forgive me as I am so forgitful."

SEVERAL GENERATIONS OF A SOUTHERN FAMILY.

(SPECIAL COLLECTIONS DEPT., EMORY UNIVERSITY)

Husbands and wives were not as forthright and uninhibited in their letters as one might expect. Civil War generations wrote in guarded fashion. Rarely did that reserve break down. One instance occurred in April 1864, when a young Southern wife wrote her soldier-husband: "My loving John, I feel like I would squeese you and hug you to death if I had a chance. You would not sleep in a week if I got my arms around you. I will make up for lost time [when you come home], so you hold yourself in readiness."

More often than not, soldiers and wives devoted much space in their letters to an attempt to combat mutual loneliness. Indiana volunteer John Craft had never been away from home before joining the Federal army. Shortly after Christmas 1861, when his wife seemed unable to control her depression, Craft wrote back: "Eliza, you must not be discouraged. Remember the Sun is never brighter than when it emerges from behind the darkest cloud. . . . I have abiding faith that all will be well yet; that our government will be sustained; that we will have yet a country, a Home, and time and opportunity alloted us to enjoy them."

The ultimate test of a soldier is battle. All else in warfare is incidental to two armies closing in combat. Northern and Southern troops may have left a good deal to be desired in camp and on the march, yet they more than compensated for those deficiencies by their overall performance on the battlefield. Sir Winston Churchill once said of Civil War soldiers: "With them, uncommon valor became a common virtue."

Letters and diaries of those men reveal that the most prevalent fear they had was not the possibility of being wounded, or even killed, but of "showing the white feather": of displaying cowardice that would bring humiliation to family and friends back home. A large percentage of

soldiers hoped for a battle wound ("a red badge of courage"), but uncertainty gripped all of them as they moved toward their first battle. Differing reactions occurred before hell literally broke loose. Soldiers remembered sweatiness, nervousness, praying fervently, "a violent pounding in the heart," "shaking hands with everyone around you," "losing control of bowels," and "urinating in pants."

Teenager Edward Edes of the 33rd Massachusetts wrote on the eve of his baptism in combat: "I have a mortal dread of the battlefield . . . I am afraid that the groans of the wounded & dying will make me shake, nevertheless I hope & trust that strength will be given me to stand up & do my duty." Edes performed admirably in his first battle but died of sickness a year later.

In marked contrast to Currier and Ives paintings and other orderly depictions of the Civil War, the actual fighting was not clean or visual at all. An assault tended to be an interrupted, accordion-like advance across a field with fixed bayonets. The attacking soldiers would rush forward a few yards, fire a volley, reload, dash several more yards, fire again, and then make a final run toward the enemy works. No matter how precise or meticulous the charge was designed to be, the whole situation tended to disintegrate the moment the battle began.

Feelings on going into combat were mixed. A Mississippian wrote of his initial battle action: "This was my first experience at being shot at, and I was as scared as the next man." One New York soldier who was part of an assault described his feelings to his sweetheart: "When we first started from our position, I thought of home, friends, and most everything else, but as soon as we entered the woods where the shells and balls were flying thick and fast, I lost all fear and thought of home and friends, and a reckless don't-care disposition seemed to take possession of me."

Men who had come from farms, factories, schools, and stores unanimously admitted that fighting was the hardest task they had ever performed. No time existed in battle for rest; food and water were practically nonexistent in the struggle. Anxiety, nervous energy, and exuberance all took

DEAD SOLDIERS ALONG
THE SUNKEN ROAD
AT ANTIETAM.

(LC)

yells and strange oaths they blindly plied the work of slaughter."

Chaos reigned everywhere. Thick, acrid smoke settled over the arena; and in the crash of musketry, the explosion of artillery fire, the screams of men fighting and dying, a soldier at best saw only what was directly in front of him. Officer casualties were high because it was customary for company, regimental, and brigade commanders to lead their men into action. Once thousands of troops became engaged in frenzied fighting, any firm control was impossible. The common soldiers were left to their own to wage the contest. Their courage and tenacity, both individually and collectively, often decided the outcome of the engagement.

In every army are men who can stand some things but not everything: soldiers whose feelings for survival override devotion to duty. When cowardice occurred in the Civil War, the steadfast ones viewed it with utter contempt. Sergeant Harold White of the 11th Iowa recalled at the battle of Shiloh that a frightened fugitive shouted as the Iowans moved into action: "Give them hell, boys! I gave them hell as long as I could!"

White observed: "Whether he had really given them any, I cannot say, but assuredly he gave them everything else he possessed, including his gun, cartridge box, and hat."

For every soldier who lacked fortitude in the Civil War, 100 others were quick to rise to the heights of courage. A call for volunteers for a dangerous task would bring shouts of response. When charging against concentrated musketry, Civil War soldiers were known to lean forward as if they were advancing into the face of a heavy rainstorm. Men jumped

such a toll that by midafternoon many soldiers were barely able to stand, much less to load and fire a gun.

No participant in the Civil War ever forgot a battle scene. It so exceeded anything they had ever witnessed that soldiers had difficulty composing word-pictures of it. Still, a Billy Yank came close to unloading all of his impressions with this account of the fighting at Gettysburg: "Foot to foot, body to body and man to man, they struggled, pushed and strived and killed. Each had rather die than yield. The mass of wounded and heaps of dead entangled the feet of the contestants, and, underneath the trampling mass, wounded men who could no longer stand, struggled, fought, shouted and killed—hatless, coatless, drowned in sweat, black with powder, red with blood, stifling in the horrid heat, parched with smoke and blind with dust, with fiendish

atop parapets to yell defiance at the enemy; they begged for the privilege of carrying the regimental colors; they took command without being told when all of the officers were disabled; they refused to leave the

JOHN WALTON ENLISTED IN AUGUST 1862 AT AGE TWENTY WITH THE 95TH OHIO VOLUNTEER INFANTRY. HE WAS CAPTURED IN JUNE 1864 AND HELD PRISONER.

(COURTESY OF DENNIS KEESEE)

field when seriously wounded; many cheered on their comrades with their final dying breath.

Soldiers North and South came to have a mutual respect for the courage and sacrifice of their opponents. After the battle of Shiloh, a Midwestern cannoneer praised the Confederates to a friend: "If we ever had a notion in our heads that those fellows couldn't shoot, it was dispelled." Another Billy Yank was even more laudatory of the Southerners in that contest. "Never did I see such men fight. When you heare . . . a man say they wont fight tell him he nows nothing bout them for wen our cannons would mow them down by hundreds others

would follow and take their plase and fight like demons."

When a shell tore off both hands of a Confederate soldier, the man stared at his two bleeding stumps and mumbled: "My Lord, that stops my fighting." Major James Waddell stated in his official report of the battle of Second Manassas that his Georgia regiment "carried into the fight over 100 men who were barefoot, many of whom left bloody foot-prints among the thorns and briars through which they rushed with Spartan courage and jubilant impetuosity, upon the ranks of the foe." Before one of the bloodiest assaults of the war, Union soldiers were so convinced of the futility of their assignment that they wrote their names and units on pieces of paper and pinned them to their shirts so that the burial details could make easier identification. One New Englander hastily wrote in his

THE WARREN BROTHERS: LEVIN AND LUTHER (L-R) SERVED IN THE 19TH BATTALION, VIRGINIA HEAVY ARTILLERY. THEY ARE SHOWN WITH THEIR FATHER, PATRICK.

(MC)

WOMEN OF THE WAR

by William Marvel

U ntil 1861, the part played by women in American wars had been only incidental. For both political and sociological reasons, that began to change almost with the opening of the guns at Fort Sumter.

Until the first half of the nineteenth century, the individ-ual family had constituted the principal unit of production in a society that was largely self-suf-ficient. Within the family, men tended to provide the raw materials while women served as the manufacturers of finished products. The evolution of industrial society had freed mil-lions of women from their roles as the producers of goods, and a simultaneous, gradual reduc-tion in the size of families somewhat lessened the burdens of motherhood. These com-bined factors allowed many women the leisure to pursue other callings. By midcentury American girls were accorded the unprecedented right to equal education in public schools, and female seminaries began springing up across the country.

Added to these societal changes was the movement toward female equality: an 1848 convention in Seneca Falls, New York, had marked the opening of the women's rights movement. That movement arose at least partly as an outgrowth of the abolitionist crusade, which usurped its momentum for another generation, but the Civil War posed an opportunity for women to express and exercise their independence. It is no surprise that the founders of the women's movement and the prominent women of the war included a disproportionate number of Quakers and Universalists, for those denominations had long since begun to shed the veil of male supremacy.

Much attention has been devoted to the women who dis-guised themselves and served under arms in the Union and Confederate armies. The lack of extensive physical examinations permitted such masquerades in

MARY ANN BICKERDYKE

(LC)

diary: "June 3, 1864, Cold Harbor. I was killed." The journal was found in the coat pocket of the dead soldier.

With the end of a battle, the surviving participants soon felt a bone-deep weari-ness. Scores of them would begin search-ing the field, nearby hospital stations, and camp for a comrade who was missing. Only rarely would he be found. Soon after darkness fell, the soldiers would sink to the ground somewhere and, in spite of the screams and moans coming from the near-by battleground, sink into a fitful sleep of exhaustion.

The aftershock of battle could be traumatizing for the survivors. A soldier from Maine tried to tell his parents what part of one battle arena contained: "I have Seen . . . men rolling in their own blood, Some Shot in one place, Some another. . . . our dead lay in the road and the Rebels in their hast to leave dragged both their bag-gage wagons and artillery over them and they lay mangled and torn to pieces so that Even friends could not tell them. You can form no idea of a battle field . . . no pen can describe it. No tongue can tell its hor-ror." Another soldier noted: "When the

far greater numbers than might have been possible in later wars, and some women inevitably saw combat: a shallow grave uncovered near the Shiloh battlefield in 1934 contained the skeletons of nine Union soldiers, one of which was identified as that of a woman.

Rare wives like Kady Brownell, of Rhode Island, actually marched openly with their husbands on the parade ground and, reputedly, into battle. Armed women, however, were relatively few, disguised or not. Far more women contributed by replacing the men who left civilian employment for the army. Particularly in the Midwest and the South, great numbers of women could be found driving teams and harvesting crops; one Iowa observer recalled seeing more women in the fields than men. North and South, women turned their energy toward the production of uniforms, equipment, and medical supplies, while still others on both sides filled vacant clerkships in government bureaus. In the North, women composed much of the labor force that engaged in the manufacture of ammunition, and dozens of them were killed in the accidental explosion of a munitions factory at Pittsburgh in September of 1862.

The single greatest service that women provided lay in the field of humanitarian relief. Within a week of the outbreak of war Dorothea Dix proposed the creation of a corps of army nurses, and she was named superintendent of those nurses. Until then the care of sick and wounded soldiers had been the domain of men alone, but the war changed all that. Northern women flocked to hospitals by the thousands, both under official auspices and, like Clara Barton, independently. An 1862 Confederate law provided for female nurses wherever possible, and Southern women rose to the formal command of large military facilities.

Elizabeth Blackwell, the first woman to earn a medical degree, drew 3,000 women to a meeting in New York two weeks after Fort Sumter fell, and that meeting led to the formation of a group that became the Sanitary Commission, which saw to the general health and comfort of the U.S. soldier. In Chicago Jane Hoge and Mary Livermore organized the Northwestern Sanitary Commission, and their most famous field agent was Mary Ann Bickerdyke, known to the soldiers of the western army as Mother Bickerdyke. She was the only woman William Sherman

would allow at the front, and when his army marched in the Grand Review in 1865 she rode a horse at the head of the Fifteenth Corps. In the South, women gathered in smaller, local relief societies devoted to the health and comfort of their men in the ranks, but the dispersion of their efforts limited their effectiveness.

Dr. Mary Walker, a young medical school graduate, began the war by volunteering in Washington hospitals. From there she moved into battlefield hospitals, and in September of 1863 she was appointed assistant surgeon of an Ohio regiment. After the war she was awarded the Medal of Honor for meritorious service.

Bold, determined souls like Barton and Walker blazed a wide path for women who wished to claim their place in society. They served as clarion examples for their sisters, and their work challenged male domination of the medical profession in particular. In postwar years the veterans did not forget the devotion of their wartime nurses, often welcoming them as honorary members of their fraternal associations, and that camaraderie may have initiated a transformation in the way American men viewed the opposite sex.

fight was over & I saw what was done, the tears then came free. To think of civilized people killing one another like beasts. One would think that the supreme ruler would put a stop to it."

Sometimes the soldiers did precisely that on a momentary basis. During the war an amazing degree of fraternization took place between men of opposing armies. Pickets often shared conversation, newspapers, tobacco, coffee, even letters from home; unauthorized truces occurred more than once because of a blackberry patch or a swimming hole discovered in the no-man's land between opposing lines.

Many soldiers found it unnatural during the long periods of inactivity to shoot at an enemy who had become an acquaintance. At one point in the long siege of Petersburg, Virginia, Private George W. Buffum of Wisconsin told his wife: "We dont shute at woune a nother unles we let woune another no before we commenc fiering. We hav orders to fier wounc in a while to ceep the pickitts in snug, than we howler take care boys we are going to fier and then we lay to until we git threw."

The Civil War had to run its bloody course so that the destiny of the United States could be determined. A bloody

were then, the Northern states would lose 4,000,000 men while the Southern states would suffer 11,000,000 casualties.

Four times more Americans were casualties at the 1862 battle of Antietam than in the 1944 D-Day invasion of France. Over 125 Civil War regiments suffered losses of 50 percent or higher in a single engagement. At Gettysburg the 1st Minnesota and 26th North Carolina each suffered 85 percent losses. Ninety-one pairs of brothers served in an Illinois regiment. Of these, 43 pairs were killed in action and 15 pairs died of sickness.

They are all gone now—the last of them died in the 1950s—but they left something for us to remember and to use. From the fractures of that war came common ties. All that the survivors on both sides endured ultimately became a common bond that brought them together. The millions of farmboys, students, and clerks

course it truly was. Almost 700,000 American soldiers of blue and gray gave their lives in the Civil War to define the nation's destiny. If civil war erupted today in America and total losses were in the same proportion to population now as they

Pickets trading. Between The lines.

With the passing years the men of blue and gray aged gracefully. Time healed most wounds and obliterated scars of mind and body.

who went home from that terrible storm of fire and blood realized that they had been witness to the greatest event of the century. As time cooled passions, shared experiences helped to forge a oneness. A postwar brotherhood took root, and it became more concrete than the ties of sectional allegiance had been.

With the passing years the men of blue and gray aged gracefully. Time healed most wounds and obliterated scars of mind and body. "Some good to the world must come from such sacrifice," a North Carolina veteran observed late in life; and when Tennessean John Mason was asked in the 1920s about his Civil War experiences, the bent and gray-haired Confederate responded: "I fired a cannon. I hope I never killed anyone."

"HOME COMING, 1865"
PAINTING BY
W. L. SHEPPARD.

(MC)

From a common pride came a common legacy, and they remain foundations of a nation of united states. Johnny Rebs and Billy Yanks demonstrated for all time how to endure, to fight, to suffer, to die, to remember, and to forgive. In the fire and ashes of a great civil war, the strength of the common folk stood supreme. Because of that, and because of them, America still lives.